To Papa,

Happy Birthday!

You can read this to me so I can know all about your big holiday

Lot of love,

Carly x

JAPAN
WORLD ADVENTURES

BY HARRIET BRUNDLE

BookLife

©2017
Book Life
King's Lynn
Norfolk PE30 4LS

ISBN: 978-1-78637-128-7

All rights reserved
Printed in Malaysia

Written by:
Harriet Brundle

Edited by:
Charlie Ogden

Designed by:
Drue Rintoul

A catalogue record for this book
is available from the British Library.

JAPAN
WORLD ADVENTURES

Words in **red** can be found in the glossary on page 24.

CONTENTS

WHERE IS JAPAN?

Japan is a country found in Asia. The capital city of Japan is Tokyo.

JAPAN

The **population** of Japan is over 127 million.
Tokyo is the biggest city in Japan.

JAPAN

PEOPLE FROM JAPAN SPEAK JAPANESE.

WEATHER AND LANDSCAPE

The weather in Japan is mostly warm. The warmest months are usually July, August and September.

MOUNT FUJI, JAPAN

Japan has lots of different landscapes. There are many mountains and the tallest mountain is called Mount Fuji.

CLOTHING

A kimono is a **traditional** robe that is worn in Japan. Kimonos are often worn on special occasions.

KIMONO

People in Japan mostly wear comfortable and **modern** clothing because of the warm weather.

RELIGION

The **religions** with the most followers in Japan are Buddhism and Shinto.

People who follow Buddhism are called Buddhists. The Buddhist place of **worship** is called a temple.

BUDDHIST TEMPLE

FOOD

Sushi is a traditional Japanese dish. It is usually made from rice and fish.

SUSHI

Noodles are a popular dish in Japan. It is said to be rude if you do not make a slurping sound when eating noodles!

AT SCHOOL

Children in Japan go to school at the age of six.
They usually go to school until they are 18 years old.

Many children learn traditional Japanese arts, such as haikus, which are a type of poetry.

AT HOME

Traditional Japanese houses are usually made out of wood. Many homes have a sliding door made out of paper, called a shoji.

SHOJI

Many homes in Japan have beautiful Japanese gardens. They usually have many different trees, flowers and ponds in them.

FAMILIES

Family members, such as parents and grandparents, often live together in Japan.

Many families and friends get together to celebrate **festivals**, such as the Cherry Blossom festival.

CHERRY BLOSSOM

PEOPLE CELEBRATE THE BEAUTY OF SPRING.

SPORT

A popular sport in Japan is sumo wrestling. Two people try to push each other out of a circle marked on the floor.

Baseball is another popular sport in Japan. Baseball is a game that is played between two teams and uses a bat and ball.

FUN FACTS

Japan is home to lots of different animals, such as koi fish, sika deer and Asian black bears.

ASIAN BLACK BEAR

KOI FISH

SIKA DEER

The Japanese tea **ceremony** is an activity that involves preparing and serving green tea. It is an important part of Japanese culture.

GLOSSARY

ceremony	a special event performed on a religious or social occasion
festivals	times when people come together to celebrate a special event
modern	something from recent or present times
population	the number of people living in a place
religions	different beliefs in a god or gods
traditional	related to very old behaviours or beliefs
worship	a religious act such as praying

INDEX

Photocredits: Abbreviations: l-left, r-right, b-bottom, t-top, c-centre, m-middle.
Front Cover l – Ronnachai Palas. Front Cover r – Aleksey Klints. 2 – Ikunl. 5 – leungchopan. 6 – TNPhotographer. 7 – Bule Sky Studio. 8 – cowardlion. 9 – imtmphoto. 10 – SasinTipchai. 11 – Sean Pavone. 12 – Tetiana Chudovska. 13 – Waraporn Chokchaiworarat. 14 – Tom Wang. 15 – sukiyaki. 16 – Takeshi Nishio. 17 – ioong. 18 – imtmphoto. 19 – Guitar photographer. 20 – J. Henning Buchholz. 21 – mTaira. 22l – gualtiero boffi. 22c – Anan Kaewkhammul. 22r – Anan Kaewkhammul. 23 – KPG_Payless. 23inset – violetblue. Images are courtesy of Shutterstock.com, unless stated otherwise. With thanks to Getty Images, Thinkstock Photo and iStockphoto.